The Vegan Vibe
Recipes Cookbook

Easy Vegan Dishes for Wellness, Flavor, and Conscious Eating

NIGELLE LORNE

DISCLAIMER

Before diving into the delicious world of *The Vegan Vibe Recipes Cookbook: Easy Vegan Dishes for Wellness, Flavor, and Conscious Eating,* please take a moment to read this important information.

General Information

The recipes and tips in this cookbook are designed to inspire and guide you on your plant-based cooking journey. While we've done our best to provide reliable and practical advice, your results may vary depending on ingredient choices, cooking techniques, and kitchen equipment.

Health and Safety

Your well-being is our priority! As you prepare your meals, always practice standard kitchen safety be mindful of sharp knives, hot surfaces, and boiling liquids. Some plant-based ingredients, such as nuts, soy, and gluten-containing grains, may cause allergic reactions or sensitivities in certain individuals. If you have any food allergies or dietary restrictions, please review each recipe carefully and consult a healthcare professional if needed.

Nutritional Information

The nutritional details provided for each recipe are estimates and may vary based on the specific brands and portion sizes you use. For the most accurate nutritional breakdown, consider consulting a registered dietitian or using a nutrition calculator tailored to your chosen ingredients.

Now that you're all set, let's get cooking! Embrace the vibrant flavors of plant-based meals and enjoy every wholesome, delicious bite.

About The Author

Nigelle Lorne is a passionate home cook and recipe creator dedicated to crafting wholesome, flavorful, and vibrant plant-based meals that are both nourishing and accessible to all. With a deep love for fresh, natural ingredients, Nigelle has curated a collection of recipes that celebrate the essence of vegan cooking where simplicity meets creativity, and every dish is a feast for the senses.

Nigelle's culinary journey began with a commitment to healthy living, sustainability, and a desire to reimagine classic flavors through a plant-based lens. Inspired by the rich diversity of global cuisines and the transformative power of food, Nigelle has spent years perfecting recipes that bring balance, nutrition, and indulgence to the table. Through continuous experimentation and a profound respect for the art of cooking, Nigelle has developed a style that is both approachable and exciting, proving that vegan meals can be just as comforting and satisfying as traditional dishes.

As a self-taught chef, Nigelle believes that cooking is more than just meal preparation it's an opportunity to nourish the body, spark creativity, and bring people together. With the firm belief that plant-based eating should be enjoyable for everyone, Nigelle's recipes are designed to be simple, flavorful, and adaptable, making it easy for both beginners and seasoned cooks to embrace a vegan lifestyle with confidence. Whether you're cooking for yourself, your family, or a gathering of friends, Nigelle's approach ensures that every meal is a celebration of good food and shared moments.

In ***The Vegan Vibe Recipes Cookbook:Easy Vegan Dishes for Wellness, Flavor, and Conscious Eating,*** **Nigelle** shares a carefully curated collection of easy-to-follow, delicious recipes that highlight the beauty of plant-based ingredients. With practical tips, innovative cooking techniques, and a focus on well-balanced meals, this cookbook invites you to discover the joy of vegan cooking, explore new flavors, and embrace a healthier, more sustainable way of eating one delicious bite at a time.

How to Use This Cookbook

Welcome to **The Vegan Vibe Recipes Cookbook:** *Easy Vegan Dishes for Wellness, Flavor, and Conscious Eating!* This cookbook is your go-to guide for creating delicious, wholesome, and satisfying plant-based meals with ease. Whether you're looking for quick weeknight dinners, meal-prepping for the week, or discovering exciting new ways to enjoy plant-based ingredients, this book is here to help. Here's how to make the most of your cookbook experience:

Start With the Basics

If you're new to plant-based cooking, begin by reading the introductory chapters. These sections will help you understand the fundamentals of vegan cuisine, from essential pantry staples to ingredient swaps that enhance flavor and nutrition. You'll also find tips for balancing meals, maximizing flavor, and making cooking an enjoyable and rewarding experience.

Explore Recipes by Meal Type

To make finding the perfect dish effortless, this cookbook is organized by meal type:

- **Breakfast Recipes:** Start your day with nourishing options like protein-packed smoothie bowls, hearty oat-based dishes, and energizing scrambles.

- **Lunch Recipes:** Enjoy vibrant, satisfying meals like nutrient-rich salads, hearty grain bowls, and flavorful wraps.

- **Dinner Recipes:** From comforting one-pot meals to elegant entrées perfect for gatherings, you'll find a variety of flavorful plant-based dishes to end your day on a high note.

Plan Your Week

This cookbook includes meal-planning tips to help you stay organized and make meal prep a breeze. You'll find a flexible **7-day meal plan** that allows you to mix and match recipes to fit your schedule. Many dishes also include **prep-ahead tips** so you can batch-cook and save time while keeping meals fresh and exciting throughout the week.

Understand the Recipe Format

Every recipe is designed to be simple and easy to follow. Here's what to expect:

- **Ingredients List:** A focus on fresh, wholesome, and easy-to-find plant-based ingredients.

- **Prep Time and Cook Time:** To help you manage your time effectively.

- **Step-by-Step Instructions:** Clear directions that make cooking stress-free, even for beginners.

- **Pro Tips:** Expert suggestions to elevate flavors, adjust seasoning, or make substitutions based on what you have on hand.

- **Storage and Reheating Notes:** Guidance on keeping leftovers fresh and delicious for future meals.

Customize Recipes to Fit Your Taste

Each recipe is thoughtfully crafted for balance and flavor, but cooking should always be **personalized to your preferences**. Feel free to experiment add extra herbs, swap vegetables, or adjust spices to match your flavor profile. The best part of plant-based cooking is its versatility, so don't be afraid to make the dishes your own.

Incorporate Healthy Choices

This cookbook emphasizes meals that are both **nutritious and flavorful**. Throughout the book, you'll find tips on incorporating more plant-based protein, boosting essential nutrients, and making smart ingredient swaps all while keeping every dish satisfying and delicious.

Embrace the Special Sections

Beyond recipes, this cookbook offers additional resources to support your plant-based journey:

- **Meal Planning Tips:** Learn how to stock your kitchen with essentials and simplify grocery shopping and meal prep.

- **Troubleshooting Guide:** Find solutions for common challenges, such as adjusting seasoning, thickening soups, or balancing textures.

- **Tips for Hosting:** Whether you're cooking for plant-based and non-vegan guests alike, discover ways to create meals that everyone will love.

Learn as You Go

If you're new to plant-based cooking, start with simpler recipes and gradually explore more advanced dishes. This cookbook is designed to **build your confidence in the kitchen**, helping you develop an intuitive understanding of plant-based ingredients and how they work together to create delicious meals.

Share the Experience

Food is meant to be shared, and plant-based meals are no exception! Whether you're cooking for yourself or preparing a meal with family and friends, take the opportunity to **enjoy the process and share your love for vibrant, plant-powered dishes**. If you find a recipe you adore, customize it to make it your own or pass it along to inspire others.

Enjoy the Journey

The Vegan Vibe Recipes Cookbook is your gateway to a world of **delicious, nourishing, and sustainable** cooking. Whether you're an experienced plant-based eater or just starting out, this book will **inspire you to cook with passion, creativity, and joy**.

Now, gather your ingredients, choose a recipe that excites you, and let's get started on your plant-based cooking adventure!

Contents

INTRODUCTION

Imagine stepping into a kitchen where the aroma of fresh herbs, roasted vegetables, and warming spices fills the air. Every pot, pan, and bowl holds the potential to create something nourishing, vibrant, and full of life. That's the magic of plant-based cooking the power to transform simple, natural ingredients into meals that are not only delicious but also deeply satisfying. Welcome to *The Vegan Vibe Recipes Cookbook* your ultimate guide to mastering the art of plant-based meals with ease, creativity, and joy!

Why Vegan? Why Now?

Whether you're a long-time vegan, just starting your plant-based journey, or simply looking to incorporate more wholesome meals into your diet, this cookbook is for you. Eating vegan isn't just about eliminating animal products it's about embracing a whole new world of flavors, textures, and nutrient-rich ingredients that fuel your body and mind. More people than ever are making the shift, not only for personal health but also for the well-being of the planet. And guess what? Vegan food has never been more exciting, accessible, and downright delicious!

What You'll Find in This Cookbook

This cookbook is more than just a collection of recipes it's a culinary adventure designed to inspire and equip you with everything you need to make incredible plant-based meals. Inside, you'll discover:

✓ A Blend of Tradition & Innovation – From classic comfort foods to modern, creative dishes, these recipes honor the past while embracing fresh, new techniques.

✓ Easy, Everyday Recipes – Whether you have 10 minutes or an hour, there's a meal for every schedule, ensuring you stay nourished no matter how busy life gets.

✓ Nutrient-Packed, Flavorful Dishes – Say goodbye to bland, boring food! Each recipe is crafted to bring out bold flavors while providing essential nutrients for optimal health.

✓ Practical Tips & Tricks – Learn how to stock a vegan pantry, meal prep efficiently, and substitute ingredients like a pro.

Cooking with Confidence & Creativity

Cooking should never feel like a chore it should be a joyful, intuitive experience! This cookbook will guide you through simple techniques, smart substitutions, and game-changing tips that will elevate your cooking skills and boost your confidence in the kitchen. Whether you're simmering a hearty stew, blending a creamy soup, or crafting the perfect plant-based burger, you'll learn how to make every meal effortlessly delicious.

Let's Get Cooking!!!!!

HOW TO START AND STICK TO GRANDMA RECIPES

Food is more than just sustenance it's culture, connection, and celebration. Whether you're cooking for yourself, your family, or a gathering of friends, these recipes are designed to bring people together over a shared love for good food. So, grab your favorite ingredients, fire up the stove, and let's dive into *The Vegan Vibe Recipes Cookbook*!

Get ready to experience plant-based cooking in a whole new way where every meal is a vibe.

How to Start and Stick to Vegan Recipes

So, you've decided to dive into the world of vegan cooking congratulations! Whether you're fully embracing a plant-based lifestyle or just looking to add more wholesome, veggie-packed meals to your routine, the key to success is **starting strong and staying consistent**.

Switching to vegan recipes isn't just about cutting out animal products; it's about discovering a **new way of cooking, eating, and enjoying food**. It's about nourishing your body with natural ingredients, exploring exciting flavors, and making meals that leave you feeling satisfied and energized. If you're wondering where to start and how to make this a lasting habit, don't worry you're in the right place!

Step 1: Set Your Intentions

Before you even step into the kitchen, ask yourself: **Why do I want to incorporate more vegan recipes into my life?**

- Is it for better health?

- A love for animals?

- To reduce your environmental impact?

- Simply to try something new and exciting?

Having a clear reason helps you stay motivated and makes the journey more enjoyable. Whether you're transitioning to a fully plant-based diet or just experimenting with a few meals a week, **every step counts**.

Step 2: Stock Your Vegan Pantry

Cooking vegan meals is much easier when you have the right ingredients on hand. Here are some **must-have staples** to keep in your kitchen:

Grains & Legumes:

✅ Quinoa, brown rice, couscous, oats

✅ Lentils, chickpeas, black beans, kidney beans

✅ Whole wheat pasta, soba noodles

Fruits & Vegetables:

✅ Leafy greens (kale, spinach, Swiss chard)

✅ Root vegetables (sweet potatoes, carrots, beets)

✅ Fresh and frozen fruits (bananas, berries, citrus)

Healthy Fats:

✅ Avocados

✅ Nuts and seeds (almonds, walnuts, chia, flaxseeds)

✅ Olive oil, coconut oil, tahini

Plant-Based Proteins:

✅ Tofu, tempeh, seitan

✅ Nutritional yeast (adds a cheesy, umami flavor!)

✅ Edamame, hummus

Flavor Boosters:

✅ Herbs and spices (turmeric, cumin, paprika, basil)

✅ Soy sauce or tamari

✅ Miso paste, coconut aminos

✅ Garlic, ginger, lemon juice, vinegar

Once your pantry is stocked, **vegan cooking becomes much easier and more fun!**

Step 3: Start with Simple, Flavorful Recipes

One of the biggest mistakes beginners make is trying to cook complex recipes right away. Instead, **start with easy, delicious meals** that require minimal effort but pack a lot of flavor. Here are some beginner-friendly ideas:

Hearty Lentil Soup – A protein-packed, one-pot meal.

Roasted Vegetable & Quinoa Bowl – A simple, nourishing dish.

Avocado Toast with Chickpeas – Quick, satisfying, and nutritious.

Coconut Curry Soup – A rich, creamy comfort meal.

"As you get more comfortable, experiment with different ingredients and seasonings to discover what you love."

Step 4: Make Meal Prep Your Best Friend

One of the best ways to stick to vegan cooking is **meal prepping**. When you have healthy, homemade meals ready to go, you're less likely to fall back on processed or non-vegan options.

- **Batch cook soups and stews** – They store well and taste even better the next day.
- **Chop veggies ahead of time** – Makes cooking faster and more convenient.
- **Prepare grains and legumes in bulk** – Having cooked rice, quinoa, or lentils in the fridge makes meals effortless.
- **Keep healthy snacks handy** – Nuts, hummus, and fresh fruits keep hunger at bay.

By prepping ahead, you'll always have a nourishing meal ready, even on busy days!

Step 5: Keep It Fun & Flexible

The key to sticking with vegan recipes long-term is to **enjoy the process!** Try new recipes, explore global cuisines, and **don't stress about being perfect**. If you slip up or crave something outside your usual plant-based routine, it's okay! Just pick up where you left off and keep going.

✹ **Experiment** – Try making your favorite non-vegan dishes plant-based.

✹ **Stay Inspired** – Follow vegan chefs, watch cooking videos, and join online communities.

✹ **Share Your Food** – Cooking for family and friends makes it even more rewarding.

Step 6: Listen to Your Body

Switching to vegan meals can bring amazing benefits more energy, better digestion, and glowing skin. But everyone's body is different, so **pay attention to how you feel**.

💡 Are you getting enough protein?

💡 Do you need more healthy fats?

💡 Are you drinking enough water?

Eating a variety of whole, nutrient-dense foods will keep you feeling your best. If needed, consider plant-based supplements like **B12, omega-3s, and iron** to ensure balanced nutrition.

Your Vegan Journey Starts Here!

The most important thing to remember is that **vegan cooking is a journey, not a destination**. Start where you are, make small changes, and most importantly **have fun in the kitchen!**

With this cookbook, you'll have **plenty of delicious, easy-to-follow recipes** to keep you inspired. So grab your ingredients, fire up the stove, and let's start cooking some magic!

CONVERSATIONAL PROMPT OR QUESTIONS

Cooking is more than just following a recipe it's about creativity, exploration, and discovering flavors that bring joy and nourishment. As you embark on your plant-based journey, here are five thought-provoking questions to help you reflect, experiment, and deepen your connection with vegan cooking:

What was your biggest misconception about vegan cooking before you started, and how has your perspective changed? Let's use that as a starting point to recreate those cherished memories in your own kitchen!

_____

_____

_____

_____

Many people assume that plant-based meals are bland, lack variety, or don't provide enough protein. As you cook through this book, take a moment to reflect on how your experience with flavors, ingredients, and nutrition evolves.

If you could recreate any traditional dish using only plant-based ingredients, what would it be and why?

_____

_____

_____

_____

One of the most exciting aspects of vegan cooking is reimagining classic dishes in a plant-based way. Whether it's a creamy pasta, a hearty stew, or a nostalgic childhood favorite, challenge yourself to craft a vegan version that's just as delicious if not better!

What's one plant-based ingredient you've discovered that you now can't live without?

_____

_____

_____

_____

Every vegan cook has that one special ingredient that elevates their meals. Maybe it's **nutritional yeast for its cheesy depth**, **aquafaba for its magic in baking**, or **coconut milk for creamy soups and curries**. As you explore new recipes, take note of the ingredients that transform your cooking.

How do you balance flavor, texture, and nutrition when creating a plant-based meal?

_____

_____

_____

_____

Great vegan cooking isn't just about eliminating animal products it's about creating bold flavors, satisfying textures, and well-rounded nutrition. Think about how you can layer spices, use different cooking methods, and combine whole foods to make every dish nourishing and exciting.

What's your go-to comfort meal when you need something warm, satisfying, and nourishing?

_____

_____

_____

_____

Comfort food is deeply personal, and vegan cooking offers endless possibilities for cozy, soul-warming meals. Whether it's a rich **lentil soup**, a creamy **butternut squash bisque**, or a hearty **chickpea and sweet potato stew**, embrace the plant-based dishes that make you feel at home.

As you work through this cookbook, let these questions inspire you to experiment, personalize recipes, and truly enjoy the process of plant-based cooking. After all, the best meals are the ones made with curiosity and love!!!

FOODS TO EAT AND AVOID FOR STAYING HEALTHY

Eating a **nutrient-rich, well-balanced vegan diet** is about more than just avoiding animal products it's about **embracing whole, plant-based foods that nourish your body and keep you energized**. Whether you're new to vegan cooking or a seasoned plant-based eater, knowing **what to include and what to avoid** can help you create delicious, wholesome meals that support your health.

Foods to Include for a Healthy Vegan Diet

To ensure your body gets all the essential nutrients, **focus on whole, minimally processed plant foods** that provide protein, fiber, healthy fats, vitamins, and minerals. Here's what to prioritize:

1. Protein-Rich Plant Foods

Many people worry about getting enough protein on a vegan diet, but **plants provide plenty!** Aim to include a variety of these protein-packed foods:

✓ **Legumes** (lentils, chickpeas, black beans, kidney beans)

✓ **Tofu, tempeh, and edamame** (excellent soy-based protein sources)

✓ **Quinoa** (a complete protein with all nine essential amino acids)

✓ **Nuts and seeds** (almonds, walnuts, chia seeds, hemp seeds, flaxseeds)

✓ **Seitan** (a high-protein meat substitute made from wheat gluten)

💡 **Pro Tip:** Pairing beans with whole grains (e.g., rice and beans) helps provide a full spectrum of essential amino acids for optimal protein intake.

2. Whole Grains for Energy & Fiber

Whole grains provide **complex carbohydrates, fiber, and essential nutrients** that support digestion and sustained energy. Choose:

✓ **Brown rice, quinoa, farro, barley**

✓ **Whole wheat pasta, whole grain bread, buckwheat**

✓ **Oats and millet**

💡 **Pro Tip:** Swap refined grains (like white rice and white bread) for whole grains to maximize fiber and nutrients.

3. Colorful Vegetables for Vitamins & Antioxidants

Vibrant, colorful vegetables provide a **wide range of vitamins, minerals, and antioxidants** that support overall health.

✅ **Leafy greens** (kale, spinach, collard greens – high in iron and calcium)

✅ **Cruciferous veggies** (broccoli, Brussels sprouts, cauliflower – great for detoxification)

✅ **Root vegetables** (sweet potatoes, carrots, beets – loaded with beta-carotene and fiber)

✅ **Bell peppers, tomatoes, zucchini, mushrooms** (rich in vitamin C, potassium, and antioxidants)

💡 **Pro Tip:** The more **colorful** your plate, the more diverse your nutrient intake!

4. Fruits for Natural Sweetness & Nutrients

Fruits provide **natural sugars, fiber, and essential vitamins** while satisfying your sweet cravings. Include:

✅ **Berries** (strawberries, blueberries, raspberries – high in antioxidants)

✅ **Bananas, oranges, and apples** (great sources of potassium and vitamin C)

✅ **Avocados** (packed with healthy fats and fiber)

✅ **Dried fruits (in moderation!)** (dates, figs, raisins – great for natural sweetness)

💡 **Pro Tip:** Pair fruit with nuts or nut butter for a balanced snack that includes **healthy fats and protein.**

5. Healthy Fats for Brain & Heart Health

Healthy fats are **essential for brain function, hormone balance, and heart health**. Prioritize these sources:

✅ **Avocados** (a creamy, nutritious fat source)

✅ **Nuts and nut butters** (almonds, cashews, walnuts, peanut butter)

✅ **Seeds** (chia, flax, hemp – great for omega-3s)

✅ **Olive oil and coconut oil** (for cooking and salad dressings)

💡 **Pro Tip:** Sprinkle chia or flaxseeds on your oatmeal or smoothies for an extra boost of **omega-3 fatty acids**.

6. Plant-Based Dairy Alternatives

Instead of traditional dairy, opt for **fortified plant-based alternatives** that provide calcium, vitamin D, and protein. Look for:

✅ **Almond, soy, oat, or cashew milk** (fortified with calcium and vitamin D)

✅ **Plant-based yogurts** (coconut, almond, or soy-based options)

✅ **Cashew or tofu-based cheeses**

💡 **Pro Tip:** **Soy milk** has the most protein of all plant-based milks, making it a great choice for smoothies and cooking.

7. Natural Sweeteners (in Moderation!)

Instead of refined sugar, opt for **natural sweeteners** like:

✅ **Maple syrup or agave nectar**

✅ **Date syrup or mashed bananas**

✅ **Coconut sugar**

💡 **Pro Tip:** While natural, these are still sugars so use them in moderation!

🚫 Foods to Avoid or Minimize.

While it's okay to enjoy treats occasionally, limiting **processed, artificial, and nutrient-poor foods** will help maintain a balanced, healthy vegan diet.

1. Highly Processed Vegan Foods

❌ Vegan junk food (store-bought cookies, chips, candy)

❌ Processed vegan meats (some have additives and excess sodium)

❌ Artificially flavored plant-based snacks

💡 **Choose homemade versions whenever possible!**

2. Refined Sugars & White Flour

❌ White bread, white pasta, and processed baked goods

❌ High-fructose corn syrup and refined white sugar

💡 **Swap for whole grains and natural sweeteners.**

3. Unhealthy Oils & Fats

❌ Hydrogenated oils and trans fats (found in some processed foods)

❌ Excessive fried foods

💡 **Opt for olive oil, avocado oil, or coconut oil instead.**

4. Alcohol & Sugary Drinks

❌ Soda, sweetened juices, energy drinks

❌ Excessive alcohol (which can interfere with nutrient absorption)

💡 **Drink water, herbal teas, or fresh fruit-infused water instead.**

VEGAN SECRET: Eat Whole, Eat Balanced, Eat Vibrantly!

A healthy vegan diet isn't about perfection it's about **making conscious choices** that nourish your body while enjoying a variety of delicious, plant-based foods.

✅ **Fill your plate with colorful, whole foods.**

✅ **Listen to your body's needs.**

✅ **Cook at home as much as possible.**

✅ **Enjoy treats in moderation!**

By focusing on **nutrient-rich, whole ingredients**, you'll not only enjoy flavorful vegan meals but also **feel your best every day!!!**

Test Your Knowledge: Vegan Nutrition & Healthy Eating

Understanding the basics of a **nutrient-rich vegan diet** is key to creating balanced, delicious meals. Take this short quiz to check your knowledge and reinforce what you've learned so far!

1. Which of the following is NOT a good source of plant-based protein?

A) Lentils

B) Tofu

C) Quinoa

D) White bread

✅ Answer: D) White bread

While lentils, tofu, and quinoa provide essential plant-based protein, white bread is a refined grain with minimal protein content.

2. Why is it important to eat a variety of colorful vegetables in a vegan diet?

A) They provide a wide range of vitamins, minerals, and antioxidants

B) They make meals look prettier but don't add much nutrition

C) They are the only source of plant-based protein

D) They replace the need for healthy fats in a balanced diet

✅ Answer: A) They provide a wide range of vitamins, minerals, and antioxidants

Eating a variety of colorful vegetables ensures diverse nutrient intake, supporting overall health and wellness.

3. Which foods should be minimized or avoided to maintain a balanced vegan diet?

A) Whole grains, legumes, and nuts

B) Processed vegan snacks, refined sugars, and trans fats

C) Leafy greens, berries, and olive oil

D) Fortified plant-based dairy alternatives

✅ Answer: B) Processed vegan snacks, refined sugars, and trans fats

While some processed vegan foods can be convenient, they often contain artificial additives, excess sugars, and unhealthy fats that don't support long-term health.

By focusing on **whole, plant-based foods and limiting highly processed options**, you'll create flavorful, nourishing meals that support your well-being. Keep exploring new ingredients, stay curious, and most importantly enjoy your vegan cooking journey!!!

MEAL PLANNING FOR BEGINNERS: A GUIDE TO EASY & STRESS-FREE VEGAN MEALS

Meal planning is one of the **best ways to stay consistent, save time, and ensure a balanced, nutritious vegan diet**. Whether you're new to plant-based eating or just looking to simplify your routine, having a plan helps you **avoid last-minute stress, reduce food waste, and make healthier choices**.

In this guide, we'll break down the essentials of meal planning and provide **practical tips to help you get started** so you can enjoy delicious, homemade vegan meals without the hassle!

Step 1: Set Your Meal Planning Goals

Before you start planning, think about what you want to achieve:

✓ Do you want to save time during busy weekdays?

✓ Are you looking to improve your nutrition and balance your meals?

✓ Do you want to reduce food waste and grocery costs?

Understanding your **personal goals** will help you create a meal plan that works for your lifestyle.

Step 2: Choose Your Approach to Meal Planning

There are different ways to plan meals pick the method that suits you best!

✅ **Full Weekly Meal Plan (Best for Beginners)**

Plan **all your meals** (breakfast, lunch, dinner, and snacks) for the entire week. This is great for **organization** and helps ensure **balanced nutrition**.

✅ **Partial Meal Plan (Best for Flexibility)**

Plan **only a few meals per week** (e.g., dinners only) and leave room for spontaneity or leftovers.

✅ **Batch Cooking & Prepping (Best for Busy Schedules)**

Prepare staple ingredients in advance (e.g., cooked grains, roasted veggies, soups, or sauces) so you can mix and match throughout the week.

Step 3: Build a Balanced Vegan Meal Plan

A well-rounded vegan meal should include:

Vegetables – Leafy greens, cruciferous veggies, root vegetables

Whole Grains – Brown rice, quinoa, oats, whole wheat pasta

Plant-Based Proteins – Lentils, chickpeas, tofu, tempeh, nuts, seeds

Healthy Fats – Avocados, olive oil, coconut milk, nut butters

Flavor Boosters – Herbs, spices, garlic, lemon, vinegar

Example Balanced Meal Formula:

✔ **1 Protein Source** + ✔ **1 Whole Grain** + ✔ **Plenty of Veggies** + ✔ **Healthy Fat**

For example: **Quinoa + Chickpeas + Roasted Veggies + Tahini Dressing**

Step 4: Plan Your Weekly Menu

Here's a simple way to structure your meal plan:

- **Breakfasts:** Quick, nutrient-dense meals (e.g., smoothies, oatmeal, tofu scrambles)
- **Lunches:** Simple and packable meals (e.g., grain bowls, soups, salads)
- **Dinners:** Satisfying, hearty dishes (e.g., stews, stir-fries, curries)
- **Snacks:** Healthy options to keep you full (e.g., nuts, hummus, fruit)

Step 5: Make a Grocery List & Shop Smart

Once your meals are planned, **create a grocery list** based on your ingredients.

- **Organize your list by category:** Produce, grains, proteins, pantry staples
- **Buy in bulk when possible** to save money on items like lentils, nuts, and rice

* **Check your kitchen first** to avoid unnecessary purchases

* **Stick to your list** to prevent impulse buying

💡 Pro Tip: Shop once a week to stay stocked while keeping ingredients fresh!

Step 6: Prep Ahead for Success

Meal prep doesn't mean cooking everything at once it's about **doing small tasks in advance** to make cooking easier.

* **Chop veggies** in advance for quick meals

* **Cook grains & legumes** in bulk for easy mixing and matching

* **Make dressings & sauces** ahead of time for instant flavor boosts

* **Prepare a big batch of soup or stew** to enjoy throughout the week

💡 Pro Tip: Store prepped ingredients in airtight containers to keep them fresh longer.

Step 7: Keep It Flexible & Fun!

Meal planning isn't about rigid rules it's about making life easier. **Leave room for changes and adjustments.**

✓ Swap meals around if needed
✓ Try new recipes to keep things exciting
✓ Use leftovers creatively (e.g., turn last night's roasted veggies into a wrap for lunch)

By **planning ahead and keeping meals simple, balanced, and delicious**, you'll enjoy stress-free cooking while nourishing your body with wholesome, plant-based meals.

✅ Start smallplan just a few meals if a full schedule feels overwhelming
✅ Use your grocery list to stay organized and budget-friendly
✅ Meal prep in a way that makes sense for your routine
✅ Have fun and experiment with new flavors!

Now, let's put this guide into action and start planning your **week of delicious vegan meals!**

7 Delicious Vegan Breakfast Recipes

Each of these **nutritious and satisfying** vegan breakfast recipes is easy to make, packed with essential nutrients, and perfect for starting your day with energy!

Creamy Chia Seed Pudding with Berries

A **rich and satisfying** breakfast loaded with **omega-3s, fiber, and antioxidants**.

Ingredients (Serves 2)

- ¼ cup chia seeds
- 1 cup unsweetened almond milk (or any plant-based milk)
- 1 tbsp maple syrup (or sweetener of choice)
- ½ tsp vanilla extract
- ½ cup mixed berries (strawberries, blueberries, raspberries)
- 1 tbsp crushed nuts or seeds (optional)

Instructions

1. In a bowl, whisk together chia seeds, almond milk, maple syrup, and vanilla extract.
2. Let the mixture sit for 5 minutes, then stir again to prevent clumping.
3. Cover and refrigerate for at least 2 hours (or overnight for best results).
4. Before serving, stir well and top with fresh berries and crushed nuts.

Prep Time: 5 minutes

Chilling Time: 2 hours (or overnight)

Servings: 2

Nutritional Information (Per Serving):

- Calories: **180**
- Protein: **5g**
- Carbohydrates: **25g**
- Fiber: **10g**
- Fats: **8g**

Tofu Scramble with Spinach & Mushrooms

A **protein-packed** alternative to scrambled eggs, loaded with **flavor and nutrition**.

Ingredients (Serves 2)

- 1 block firm tofu, crumbled
- 1 tbsp olive oil
- ½ cup mushrooms, sliced
- 1 cup fresh spinach
- ¼ tsp turmeric powder
- ½ tsp garlic powder
- Salt & black pepper, to taste
- 1 tbsp nutritional yeast (optional, for a cheesy flavor)
- 1 slice whole-grain toast (optional, for serving)

Instructions

1. Heat olive oil in a pan over medium heat.
2. Add mushrooms and sauté for 2–3 minutes until soft.
3. Stir in crumbled tofu, turmeric, garlic powder, salt, and pepper.
4. Cook for about 5 minutes, stirring occasionally.
5. Add spinach and cook for another 2 minutes until wilted.
6. Sprinkle with nutritional yeast and serve warm with toast.

Prep Time: 5 minutes

Cooking Time: 10 minutes

Servings: 2

Nutritional Information (Per Serving):

- Calories: **220**
- Protein: **15g**
- Carbohydrates: **12g**
- Fiber: **4g**
- Fats: **12g**

Banana Peanut Butter Overnight Oats

A **no-cook, grab-and-go** breakfast that's **creamy, filling, and packed with fiber**.

Ingredients (Serves 1)

- ½ cup rolled oats
- ¾ cup almond milk
- 1 tbsp peanut butter
- ½ banana, mashed
- ½ tsp cinnamon
- 1 tsp maple syrup (optional)
- 1 tbsp chopped nuts (optional)

Instructions

1. In a jar, combine oats, almond milk, peanut butter, mashed banana, cinnamon, and maple syrup.
2. Stir well, cover, and refrigerate overnight.
3. In the morning, stir again and top with chopped nuts if desired.

Prep Time: 5 minutes

Chilling Time: Overnight

Servings: 1

Nutritional Information (Per Serving):

- Calories: **310**
- Protein: **10g**
- Carbohydrates: **45g**
- Fiber: **8g**
- Fats: **12**

Avocado Toast with Cherry Tomatoes & Hemp Seeds

A **simple yet nutrient-dense** breakfast full of **healthy fats and fiber**.

Ingredients (Serves 1)

- 1 slice whole-grain bread
- ½ avocado, mashed
- 5 cherry tomatoes, sliced
- 1 tbsp hemp seeds
- Salt & black pepper, to taste
- ½ tsp lemon juice

Instructions

1. Toast the whole-grain bread until crispy.
2. Spread mashed avocado evenly over the toast.
3. Top with sliced cherry tomatoes and sprinkle with hemp seeds.
4. Season with salt, black pepper, and a squeeze of lemon juice.

Prep Time: 5 minutes

Cooking Time: 2 minutes

Servings: 1

Nutritional Information (Per Serving):

- Calories: **250**
- Protein: **7g**
- Carbohydrates: **25g**
- Fiber: **8g**
- Fats: **14g**

Green Power Smoothie

Ingredients (Serves 1)

- 1 cup spinach
- 1 banana
- ½ avocado
- 1 tbsp chia seeds
- 1 cup almond milk
- 1 tsp maple syrup (optional)

Instructions

1. Add all ingredients to a blender.
2. Blend until smooth and creamy.
3. Pour into a glass and enjoy immediately.

Prep Time: 5 minutes

Servings: 1

Nutritional Information (Per Serving):

- Calories: **280**
- Protein: **6g**
- Carbohydrates: **38g**
- Fiber: **9g**
- Fats: **12g**

A **nutrient-rich** smoothie filled with **greens, healthy fats, and plant-based protein**.

Buckwheat Pancakes with Maple Syrup & Nuts

A **gluten-free**, **high-fiber** pancake recipe that's light and fluffy!

Ingredients (Serves 2)

- 1 cup buckwheat flour
- 1 tbsp flaxseed meal + 3 tbsp water (egg replacement)
- 1 cup almond milk
- 1 tbsp maple syrup
- 1 tsp baking powder
- ½ tsp cinnamon
- 1 tbsp crushed walnuts (for topping)

Instructions

1. Mix flaxseed meal and water in a small bowl; let sit for 5 minutes.
2. In a larger bowl, combine buckwheat flour, baking powder, and cinnamon.
3. Add almond milk, flax mixture, and maple syrup; mix until smooth.
4. Heat a non-stick pan over medium heat and cook pancakes for 2–3 minutes per side.
5. Serve warm with crushed walnuts and extra maple syrup.

Prep Time: 5 minutes

Cooking Time: 10 minutes

Servings: 2

Nutritional Information (Per Serving):

- Calories: **280**
- Protein: **8g**
- Carbohydrates: **48g**
- Fiber: **6g**
- Fats: **6g**

Vegan Breakfast Burrito

A **savory, protein-rich** breakfast wrap that's perfect for meal prep.

Ingredients (Serves 2)

- 2 whole wheat tortillas
- ½ block firm tofu, crumbled
- ¼ cup black beans
- ½ cup spinach
- ¼ tsp turmeric
- ½ tsp garlic powder
- 1 tbsp salsa

Instructions

1. Heat a pan and sauté crumbled tofu with turmeric and garlic powder.
2. Add black beans and spinach, cooking until warmed through.
3. Spoon mixture into tortillas, top with salsa, and wrap.

Prep Time: 5 minutes

Cooking Time: 10 minutes

Servings: 2

Nutritional Information (Per Serving):

- Calories: **320**
- Protein: **15g**
- Carbohydrates: **45g**
- Fiber: **10g**
- Fats: **8**

Weekly Vegan Breakfast Meal Prep Guide

Planning and prepping your breakfasts in advance can save **time, reduce stress, and ensure a nutritious start to your day**. This guide provides a structured plan to help you **prepare your meals efficiently** while keeping variety and flavor in your morning routine.

How to Meal Prep Vegan Breakfasts

✅ **Choose 3–4 recipes for the week** to maintain variety.

✅ **Batch prep ingredients** to save time (e.g., cook oats, chop fruits, or make smoothie packs).

✅ **Store meals properly** in airtight containers for freshness.

✅ **Use freezer-friendly options** like muffins, pancakes, and smoothie packs for longer storage.

7-Day Vegan Breakfast Meal Plan + Prep Schedule

Monday: Chia Seed Pudding with Berries

Prep:

- Mix chia seeds, almond milk, maple syrup, and vanilla the night before.

- Store in jars and refrigerate overnight.

- In the morning, top with fresh berries and nuts.

Storage:

- Stays fresh in the fridge for up to **4 days**.

Tuesday: Tofu Scramble with Spinach & Mushrooms

Prep:

- Crumble tofu and chop mushrooms the night before.

- Store separately in airtight containers.

- In the morning, cook everything in **5–7 minutes**.

Storage:

- Cooked tofu scramble stays fresh for **3 days** in the fridge.

Wednesday: Overnight Oats with Peanut Butter & Banana

Prep:

- Combine oats, almond milk, peanut butter, mashed banana, and cinnamon in a jar.
- Refrigerate overnight for a grab-and-go meal.

Storage:

- Keeps in the fridge for **up to 5 days**.

Thursday: Avocado Toast with Cherry Tomatoes & Hemp Seeds

Prep:

- Slice cherry tomatoes and store in the fridge.
- Mash avocado with lemon juice and store separately.
- Toast bread fresh in the morning and assemble quickly.

Storage:

- Mashed avocado lasts **1–2 days** with lemon juice.

Friday: Green Power Smoothie

Prep:

- Pre-portion spinach, banana, avocado, and chia seeds into **smoothie packs** (freezer-safe bags).
- In the morning, just blend with almond milk.

Storage:

- Smoothie packs last **1 month** in the freezer.

Saturday: Buckwheat Pancakes with Maple Syrup & Nuts

Prep:

- Make pancakes in advance and store in the fridge or freezer.

- Reheat in a toaster or microwave.

Storage:

- Refrigerate for **3 days** or freeze for **1 month**.

Sunday: Vegan Breakfast Burrito

Prep:

- Cook tofu scramble and beans ahead of time.

- Store in tortillas, wrap tightly, and refrigerate or freeze.

- Reheat in the morning and add salsa before serving.

Storage:

- Refrigerate for **3 days** or freeze for **1 month**.

Final Meal Prep Tips

✓ **Batch Prep:** Make 2–3 servings of each meal at once.

✓ **Use Jars for Storage:** Mason jars work great for overnight oats and chia pudding.

✓ **Keep Breakfasts Balanced:** Include fiber, protein, and healthy fats in each meal.

✓ **Make Freezer-Friendly Options:** Pancakes, burritos, and smoothie packs are great for busy mornings.

Shopping List for the Week

Fresh Produce

✓ Spinach
✓ Mushrooms
✓ Avocado
✓ Bananas
✓ Cherry tomatoes

✓ Mixed berries
✓ Lemon

Pantry Staples

✓ Chia seeds
✓ Rolled oats
✓ Peanut butter
✓ Flaxseeds

✓ Hemp seeds
✓ Whole wheat tortillas
✓ Maple syrup
✓ Nutritional yeast
✓ Almond milk

7-Day Vegan Lunch Meal Plan

Quinoa & Chickpea Salad

Ingredients:

- 1 cup cooked quinoa
- 1 can chickpeas, drained and rinsed
- ½ cucumber, diced
- ½ red bell pepper, diced
- ¼ red onion, finely chopped
- ¼ cup parsley, chopped
- 2 tbsp olive oil
- 1 tbsp lemon juice
- Salt & pepper to taste

Instructions:

1. Cook quinoa according to package instructions and let it cool.
2. In a large bowl, mix all ingredients together.
3. Drizzle with olive oil and lemon juice. Toss well.
4. Serve fresh or store in the fridge.

Prep Time: 10 minutes
Cooking Time: 15 minutes
Servings: 2
Storage: Stays fresh in the fridge for up to **4 days**.
Nutritional Info (per serving): ~320 kcal, 12g protein, 45g carbs, 10g fat

Lentil Soup with Spinach & Carrots

Ingredients:

- 1 cup red lentils
- 4 cups vegetable broth
- 1 carrot, diced
- 1 onion, chopped
- 2 cloves garlic, minced
- 1 tsp cumin
- 1 tsp turmeric
- 2 cups fresh spinach
- 1 tbsp olive oil
- Salt & pepper to taste

Instructions:

1. Heat olive oil in a pot. Sauté onions and garlic until fragrant.
2. Add carrots, lentils, vegetable broth, and spices. Bring to a boil.
3. Simmer for 25 minutes, stirring occasionally.
4. Stir in spinach and cook for 5 more minutes.
5. Serve warm.

Prep Time: 10 minutes
Cooking Time: 30 minutes
Servings: 3
Storage: Refrigerate for **4 days** or freeze for **1 month**.
Nutritional Info (per serving): ~290 kcal, 18g protein, 40g carbs, 6g fat

Grilled Veggie & Hummus Wrap

Ingredients:

- 1 whole wheat tortilla
- ¼ cup hummus
- ½ zucchini, sliced
- ½ red bell pepper, sliced
- ½ cup mushrooms, sliced
- 1 tsp olive oil
- ½ tsp smoked paprika
- ½ cup spinach

Instructions:

1. Heat olive oil in a pan and grill zucchini, peppers, and mushrooms. Season with paprika.
2. Spread hummus over the tortilla.
3. Layer grilled veggies and spinach.
4. Wrap tightly and serve or store.

Prep Time: 10 minutes

Cooking Time: 10 minutes

Servings: 1

Storage: Refrigerate for **2 days**.

Nutritional Info (per serving): ~340 kcal, 10g protein, 50g carbs, 12g fat

Chickpea & Avocado Sandwich

Ingredients:

- 1 can chickpeas, drained and mashed
- ½ avocado, mashed
- 1 tbsp lemon juice
- 1 tbsp tahini
- 2 slices whole-grain bread
- ½ tsp garlic powder
- ½ tsp black pepper
- ½ cup lettuce

Instructions:

1. Mix mashed chickpeas, avocado, lemon juice, tahini, garlic powder, and black pepper.

2. Spread mixture over whole-grain bread.

3. Add lettuce, assemble sandwich, and serve.

Prep Time: 10 minutes

Cooking Time: 0 minutes

Servings: 1

Storage: Refrigerate filling for **2 days**.

Nutritional Info (per serving): ~380 kcal, 15g protein, 45g carbs, 14g fat

Vegan Buddha Bowl

Ingredients:

- ½ cup cooked brown rice

- ½ cup roasted sweet potatoes

- ½ cup steamed broccoli

- ¼ cup black beans

- 1 tbsp tahini dressing

- ½ avocado, sliced

Instructions:

1. Assemble all ingredients in a bowl.

2. Drizzle with tahini dressing.

3. Serve fresh or store in the fridge.

Prep Time: 10 minutes

Cooking Time: 20 minutes

Servings: 2

Storage: Refrigerate for **3 days**.

Nutritional Info (per serving): ~400 kcal, 16g protein, 55g carbs, 12g fat

Creamy Tomato & Basil Pasta

Ingredients:

- 1 cup whole wheat pasta

- ½ cup tomato sauce

- ¼ cup coconut milk

- 1 tbsp nutritional yeast

- ½ tsp garlic powder

- ½ tsp dried basil

- ½ cup cherry tomatoes, halved

Instructions:

1. Cook pasta according to package instructions.

2. In a pan, heat tomato sauce and coconut milk. Stir in nutritional yeast and spices.

3. Add cooked pasta and cherry tomatoes. Toss well.

4. Serve warm.

Prep Time: 10 minutes

Cooking Time: 15 minutes

Servings: 2

Storage: Refrigerate for **3 days**.

Nutritional Info (per serving): ~420 kcal, 14g protein, 60g carbs, 10g fat

Spicy Black Bean & Quinoa Chili

Ingredients:

- ½ cup cooked quinoa
- 1 can black beans, drained
- 1 cup diced tomatoes
- ½ onion, chopped
- 1 clove garlic, minced
- ½ tsp cumin
- ½ tsp smoked paprika
- 1 cup vegetable broth

Instructions:

1. Heat a pot and sauté onion and garlic.
2. Add black beans, tomatoes, quinoa, spices, and vegetable broth.
3. Simmer for 20 minutes, stirring occasionally.
4. Serve hot.

Prep Time: 10 minutes

Cooking Time: 20 minutes

Servings: 3

Storage: Refrigerate for **4 days** or freeze for **1 month**.

Nutritional Info (per serving): ~350 kcal, 17g protein, 50g carbs, 8g fat

Weekly Vegan Lunch Meal Prep Guide

A well-planned lunch keeps you energized and satisfied throughout the day. By prepping in advance, you can enjoy **delicious, nutrient-packed meals** with minimal daily effort. This guide provides a structured plan to make meal prepping **efficient, diverse, and flavorful**.

How to Meal Prep Vegan Lunches

✓ **Choose 3–4 recipes** to maintain variety throughout the week.

✓ **Batch cook grains and proteins** to save time.

✓ Use **airtight containers** for freshness and easy storage.

✓ **Incorporate freezer-friendly meals** for quick, ready-to-go options.

7-Day Vegan Lunch Meal Plan + Prep Schedule

Monday: Chickpea Salad

Prep:

• Cook quinoa ahead of time.

• Chop cucumbers, bell peppers, onions, and parsley.

• Toss everything with olive oil and lemon juice for easy serving.

Storage:

• Stays fresh in the fridge for **4 days**.

Tuesday: Lentil Soup with Spinach & Carrots

Prep:

• Sauté onions, garlic, and carrots.

• Add lentils, vegetable broth, and spices; simmer.

• Store in portioned containers for quick reheating.

Storage:

• Refrigerate for **4 days** or freeze for **1 month**.

Wednesday: Grilled Veggie & Hummus Wrap

Prep:

• Grill zucchini, mushrooms, and bell peppers in advance.

• Store hummus and grilled veggies separately.

• Assemble the wrap fresh for the best texture.

Storage:

• Refrigerate for **2 days**.

Thursday: Chickpea & Avocado Sandwich

Prep:

• Mash chickpeas and avocado together with tahini and lemon juice.

• Store mixture separately and assemble sandwiches fresh.

Storage:

• Chickpea filling lasts **2 days** in the fridge.

Friday: Vegan Buddha Bowl

Prep:

• Cook brown rice in advance.

• Roast sweet potatoes and steam broccoli.

• Store all ingredients separately and assemble when ready to eat.

Storage:

• Keeps fresh in the fridge for **3 days**.

Saturday: Creamy Tomato & Basil Pasta

Prep:

• Cook whole wheat pasta in advance.

• Prepare the tomato-coconut sauce and store separately.

• Combine and reheat when serving.

Storage:

• Stays fresh in the fridge for **3 days**.

Sunday: Spicy Black Bean & Quinoa Chili

Prep:

• Cook quinoa ahead of time.

• Sauté onions and garlic, then add black beans, tomatoes, and spices.

• Simmer, then portion into containers.

Storage:

• Refrigerate for **4 days** or freeze for **1 month**.

Final Meal Prep Tips for Lunches

✓ **Batch Cook:** Make multiple servings at once to save time.

✓ **Use Airtight Containers:** Helps meals stay fresh longer.

✓ **Balance Your Meals:** Include protein, fiber, and healthy fats.

✓ **Plan Ahead:** Choose meals that store well for easy grab-and-go lunches.

Shopping List for the Week

Fresh Produce

✓ Cucumbers

✓ Bell peppers

✓ Red onion

✓ Carrots

✓ Cherry tomatoes

✓ Spinach

✓ Avocado

✓ Sweet potatoes

✓ Broccoli

✓ Parsley

✓ Garlic

✓ Lemons

Pantry Staples

✓ Quinoa

✓ Chickpeas (canned or cooked)

✓ Black beans

✓ Red lentils

✓ Whole wheat tortillas

✓ Whole wheat pasta

✓ Hummus

✓ Tomato sauce

✓ Coconut milk

✓ Tahini

✓ Nutritional yeast

✓ Olive oil

✓ Vegetable broth

✓ Spices (cumin, turmeric, smoked paprika, garlic powder)

*This **weekly vegan lunch plan** makes it easy to enjoy **healthy, plant-based meals** with minimal effort. Stay prepared, stay nourished, and enjoy every bite!*

7-Day Vegan Dinner Meal Plan

Sweet Potato & Black Bean Tacos

Ingredients:

- 1 large sweet potato, diced
- 1 can black beans, drained and rinsed
- 1 tsp olive oil
- ½ tsp cumin
- ½ tsp smoked paprika
- ½ tsp garlic powder
- 4 small corn tortillas
- ¼ cup chopped cilantro
- ½ avocado, sliced
- 2 tbsp salsa

Instructions:

1. Preheat oven to 400°F (200°C). Toss sweet potatoes with olive oil and spices. Roast for 20 minutes.
2. Heat black beans in a pan for 5 minutes.
3. Warm tortillas and assemble tacos with sweet potatoes, beans, avocado, and salsa.
4. Garnish with cilantro and serve.

Prep Time: 10 minutes
Cooking Time: 20 minutes
Servings: 2
Storage: Store components separately in the fridge for **3 days**.
Nutritional Info (per serving): ~420 kcal, 14g protein, 65g carbs, 10g fat

Coconut Curry with Chickpeas & Spinach

Ingredients:

- 1 can chickpeas, drained
- 1 cup coconut milk
- 1 cup diced tomatoes
- 1 cup spinach
- ½ onion, chopped
- 1 clove garlic, minced
- 1 tsp curry powder
- ½ tsp turmeric
- ½ tsp cumin
- 1 tsp olive oil

Instructions:

1. Heat olive oil in a pan. Sauté onions and garlic until soft.
2. Add chickpeas, tomatoes, coconut milk, and spices. Simmer for 15 minutes.
3. Stir in spinach and cook for another 5 minutes.
4. Serve warm with rice or quinoa.

Prep Time: 10 minutes
Cooking Time: 20 minutes
Servings: 2
Storage: Refrigerate for **3 days** or freeze for **1 month**.
Nutritional Info (per serving): ~450 kcal, 18g protein, 50g carbs, 18g fat

Lentil & Vegetable Stir-Fry

Ingredients:

- 1 cup cooked lentils
- 1 cup mixed vegetables (carrots, bell peppers, broccoli)
- 1 tbsp soy sauce
- 1 tsp sesame oil
- ½ tsp ginger, minced
- 1 clove garlic, minced
- ½ cup cooked brown rice

Instructions:

1. Heat sesame oil in a pan. Sauté garlic and ginger.
2. Add vegetables and cook for 5 minutes.
3. Stir in lentils, soy sauce, and brown rice. Cook for another 3 minutes.
4. Serve warm.

Prep Time: 10 minutes

Cooking Time: 10 minutes

Servings: 2

Storage: Refrigerate for **3 days**.

Nutritional Info (per serving): ~400 kcal, 20g protein, 55g carbs, 8g fat

Vegan Stuffed Peppers

Ingredients:

- 2 bell peppers, halved and seeds removed
- ½ cup cooked quinoa
- ½ cup black beans
- ½ cup diced tomatoes
- ½ tsp cumin
- ½ tsp smoked paprika
- 1 tsp olive oil

Instructions:

1. Preheat oven to 375°F (190°C).
2. Mix quinoa, black beans, tomatoes, and spices in a bowl.
3. Stuff the peppers with the mixture and drizzle with olive oil.
4. Bake for 25 minutes. Serve warm.

Prep Time: 10 minutes

Cooking Time: 25 minutes

Servings: 2

Storage: Refrigerate for **3 days**.

Nutritional Info (per serving): ~370 kcal, 14g protein, 50g carbs, 9g fat

Mushroom & Spinach Pasta

Ingredients:

- 1 cup whole wheat pasta
- ½ cup mushrooms, sliced
- 1 cup spinach
- 1 clove garlic, minced
- ½ cup unsweetened almond milk
- 1 tbsp nutritional yeast
- ½ tsp black pepper
- 1 tsp olive oil

Instructions:

1. Cook pasta according to package instructions.
2. Heat olive oil in a pan. Sauté garlic and mushrooms.
3. Add spinach, almond milk, nutritional yeast, and black pepper. Simmer for 5 minutes.
4. Toss in pasta and mix well. Serve warm.

Prep Time: 10 minutes

Cooking Time: 15 minutes

Servings: 2

Storage: Refrigerate for **3 days**.

Nutritional Info (per serving): ~420 kcal, 15g protein, 60g carbs, 10g fat

Vegan Chili with Red Beans

Ingredients:

- 1 can red kidney beans, drained
- 1 can diced tomatoes
- ½ onion, chopped
- 1 clove garlic, minced
- 1 tsp cumin
- ½ tsp smoked paprika
- ½ cup vegetable broth

Instructions:

1. Heat a pot and sauté onion and garlic.
2. Add beans, tomatoes, spices, and broth. Simmer for 20 minutes.
3. Serve warm with brown rice or quinoa.

Prep Time: 10 minutes

Cooking Time: 20 minutes

Servings: 2

Storage: Refrigerate for **4 days** or freeze for **1 month**.

Nutritional Info (per serving): ~390 kcal, 17g protein, 55g carbs, 7g fat

Baked Tofu with Roasted Vegetables

Ingredients:

- 1 block firm tofu, cubed
- 1 cup mixed vegetables (carrots, zucchini, bell peppers)
- 1 tbsp soy sauce
- 1 tsp olive oil
- ½ tsp black pepper

Instructions:

1. Preheat oven to 375°F (190°C).
2. Toss tofu with soy sauce and black pepper.
3. Toss vegetables with olive oil.
4. Spread tofu and vegetables on a baking tray. Bake for 25 minutes.
5. Serve warm.

Prep Time: 10 minutes
Cooking Time: 25 minutes
Servings: 2
Storage: Refrigerate for **3 days**.
Nutritional Info (per serving): ~410 kcal, 22g protein, 50g carbs, 12g fat

Weekly Vegan Dinner Meal Prep Guide

A well-balanced dinner helps you **unwind and refuel** at the end of the day. By prepping meals in advance, you can enjoy **flavorful, nutrient-packed dishes** with ease. This guide provides a **structured plan** for an effortless dinner routine.

How to Meal Prep Vegan Dinners

✅ **Choose 3–4 recipes** to keep variety in your week.

✅ **Batch cook grains, beans, and roasted veggies** for efficiency.

✅ **Use airtight containers** to keep meals fresh.

✅ **Opt for freezer-friendly meals** to save time on busy nights.

7-Day Vegan Dinner Meal Plan + Prep Schedule

Monday: Sweet Potato & Black Bean Tacos

Prep:

• Roast sweet potatoes with olive oil and spices.

• Heat black beans and store them separately.

• Chop avocado and cilantro ahead of time.

Storage:

• Store all components separately in the fridge for **3 days**.

Tuesday: Coconut Curry with Chickpeas & Spinach

Prep:

• Sauté onions and garlic, then simmer with chickpeas, tomatoes, and coconut milk.

• Store curry in portioned containers for easy reheating.

Storage:

• Refrigerate for **3 days** or freeze for **1 month**.

Wednesday: Lentil & Vegetable Stir-Fry

Prep:

• Cook lentils and brown rice in advance.

• Chop vegetables for quicker cooking.

• Store everything separately and stir-fry when ready to eat.

Storage:

• Refrigerate for **3 days**.

Thursday: Vegan Stuffed Peppers

Prep:

• Cook quinoa and mix with black beans, diced tomatoes, and spices.

• Stuff peppers and store them in the fridge until baking.

Storage:

• Refrigerate for **3 days**.

Friday: Mushroom & Spinach Pasta

Prep:

• Cook whole wheat pasta in advance.

• Sauté mushrooms and spinach with garlic and almond milk.

• Store sauce separately and combine when serving.

Storage:

• Keeps fresh in the fridge for **3 days**.

Saturday: Vegan Chili with Red Beans

Prep:

• Cook kidney beans and mix with tomatoes, spices, and broth.

• Portion into containers for easy reheating.

Storage:

• Refrigerate for **4 days** or freeze for **1 month**.

Sunday: Baked Tofu with Roasted Vegetables

Prep:

• Cube tofu and marinate with soy sauce and spices.

• Chop vegetables and store separately.

• Bake everything fresh or prepare in advance for reheating.

Storage:

• Refrigerate for **3 days**.

Final Meal Prep Tips for Dinners

✓ **Batch Cook:** Make multiple servings at once to save time.

✓ **Use Airtight Containers:** Keeps meals fresh longer.

✓ **Balance Your Plate:** Include protein, fiber, and healthy fats.

✓ **Plan Ahead:** Choose meals that store well for easy reheating.

Shopping List for the Week

Fresh Produce

✓ Sweet potatoes

✓ Bell peppers

✓ Zucchini

✓ Carrots

✓ Broccoli

✓ Spinach

✓ Mushrooms

✓ Avocado

✓ Onion

✓ Garlic

✓ Cilantro

Pantry Staples

✓ Quinoa

✓ Brown rice

✓ Lentils

✓ Black beans

✓ Red kidney beans

✓ Chickpeas

✓ Whole wheat pasta

✓ Corn tortillas

✓ Coconut milk

✓ Diced tomatoes

✓ Nutritional yeast

✓ Soy sauce

✓ Olive oil

✓ Vegetable broth

✓ Spices (cumin, turmeric, smoked paprika, garlic powder, black pepper)

*With this **weekly vegan dinner plan**, you'll enjoy **easy, nourishing meals** while saving time in the kitchen. Happy cooking!* 🌿🍽️✨

CONCLUSION

As we turn the final page of **The Vegan Vibe Recipes Cookbook:** *Easy Vegan Dishes for Wellness, Flavor, and Conscious Eating,* let's take a moment to reflect on what these recipes truly represent. Each dish you've explored here is more than just a meal it's a step toward a more compassionate, sustainable, and mindful way of living. Vegan cooking, at its heart, is about nourishing your body, delighting your taste buds, and making choices that align with your values. This cookbook is a celebration of that journey, offering simple, flavorful dishes that make wellness and conscious eating accessible to everyone.

The beauty of these vegan recipes lies in their simplicity. They remind us that delicious, nourishing food doesn't have to be complicated or time-consuming. With just a few wholesome ingredients, you can create meals that are as kind to the planet as they are to your health. Whether it's a hearty stew simmering on the stove, a vibrant salad bursting with color, or a decadent dessert made without dairy, each recipe is a testament to the power of plant-based eating.

But these recipes are more than just instructions on a page they are an invitation to embrace a lifestyle. Vegan cooking isn't just about what you eat; it's about the stories you share, the values you uphold, and the connections you make. Perhaps you'll recall the first time you swapped an ingredient to make a dish vegan, or the joy of watching a loved one savor a plant-based meal for the first time. These are the moments that make cooking meaningful, and they are yours to create and cherish.

Now, it's your turn to carry this vibe forward. Cook these meals not just to fill plates but to fill hearts with love, with purpose, and with the joy of knowing you're making a difference. Share them with family and friends, and in doing so, create new memories around your table. Pass these recipes along, along with the stories and values that make them special. Teach others how to whip up a quick vegan stir-fry or bake a batch of cruelty-free cookies, and watch as your kitchen becomes a place where wellness, flavor, and conscious eating come together.

And remember, vegan cooking is as flexible as it is forgiving. Feel free to tweak these recipes to suit your tastes, dietary needs, or whatever ingredients you have on hand. The spirit of veganism is about creativity and compassion, so make each dish your own. Whether you're a seasoned vegan or just beginning your plant-based journey, these recipes are here to inspire you, nourish you, and remind you that every meal is an opportunity to live with intention.

So, as you close this book, know that the journey doesn't end here. Let your kitchen be a place where tradition meets innovation, where every bite is a celebration of life, and where the vibe is always vegan.

GRATITUDE

As you turn the final pages of **The Vegan Vibe Recipes Cookbook:** *Easy Vegan Dishes for Wellness, Flavor, and Conscious Eating,* my heart swells with gratitude and appreciation. Creating this cookbook has been a labor of love, filled with countless hours of testing, tweaking, and savoring meals that bring not only nourishment but also a deep sense of purpose and joy. This book is the result of dedication, creativity, and the incredible support of the people around me—those who believe in the power of plant-based eating to transform our lives and the world.

To My Readers

Thank you for welcoming this cookbook into your kitchen and for trusting me with your culinary adventures. Your enthusiasm for embracing vegan cooking, whether you're a seasoned plant-based eater or just beginning your journey, inspired every recipe in this book. I hope these dishes become staples in your home, bringing you the same sense of wellness, flavor, and conscious connection that they brought me while creating them. I look forward to hearing about your experiences and how these recipes become cherished parts of your daily life.

To My Family and Friends

Your endless support has been my foundation throughout this journey. From taste-testing countless vegan creations to providing honest feedback, your input has been invaluable. Thank you for cheering me on, for embracing my vegan lifestyle with open hearts, and for enjoying the meals that emerged from my kitchen experiments. To those who shared both compliments and constructive criticism with a smile, I am deeply grateful you've helped shape this cookbook into what it is today.

To the Vegan Cooking Community

To the home cooks, culinary enthusiasts, and creators who share their love for vegan cooking, thank you for inspiring me along the way. Online communities, social media groups, and fellow vegan recipe developers have been a constant source of ideas, encouragement, and innovation. Your passion for plant-based living and your creativity in the kitchen have fueled my own exploration and growth as a cook and as a person.

To the Tradition of Vegan Cooking

A special acknowledgment to the timeless art of vegan cooking, which has brought people together in the name of compassion, health, and sustainability. From hearty stews to innovative plant-based dishes, the vegan kitchen has become a cornerstone of wellness and conscious eating, and I am humbled to contribute to its legacy.

As you embark on your own vegan culinary journey, I hope this cookbook serves as a trusted companion, helping you create delicious, nourishing meals with ease. Cooking is not just about the food—it's about the memories made around the table, the values we uphold, and the positive impact we can have on ourselves and the planet. So, embrace the process, experiment with flavors, and most importantly, enjoy every step of the way.

With heartfelt gratitude,

NIGELLE LORNE

meal planner

date

sunday				
monday				
tuesday				
wednesday				
thursday				
friday				
saturday				

notes

meal planner

date

sunday			
monday			
tuesday			
wednesday			
thursday			
friday			
saturday			

notes

meal planner

date

sunday				
monday				
tuesday				
wednesday				
thursday				
friday				
saturday				

notes

meal planner

date

sunday				
monday				
tuesday				
wednesday				
thursday				
friday				
saturday				

notes

meal planner

date

sunday				
monday				
tuesday				
wednesday				
thursday				
friday				
saturday				

notes

meal planner

date

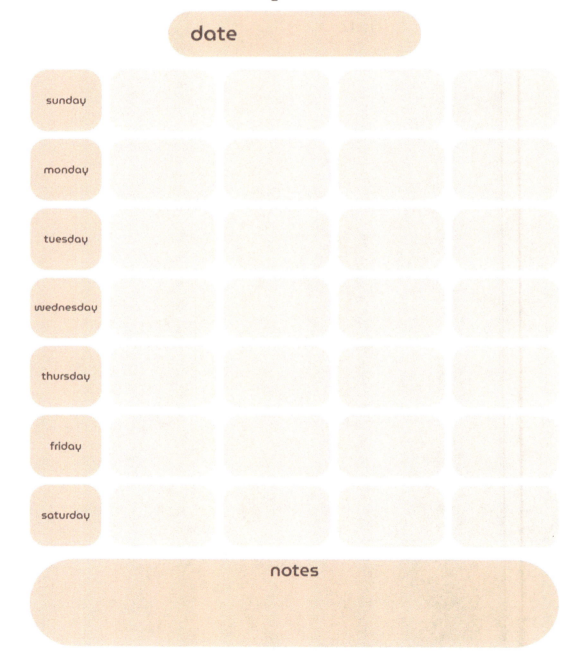

sunday				
monday				
tuesday				
wednesday				
thursday				
friday				
saturday				

notes

meal planner

date

sunday				
monday				
tuesday				
wednesday				
thursday				
friday				
saturday				

notes

meal planner

date

sunday				
monday				
tuesday				
wednesday				
thursday				
friday				
saturday				

notes

meal planner

date

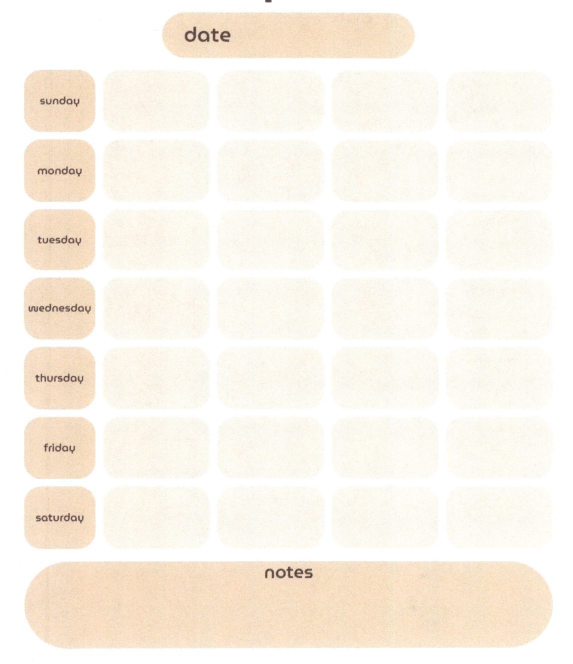

sunday				
monday				
tuesday				
wednesday				
thursday				
friday				
saturday				

notes

meal planner

date

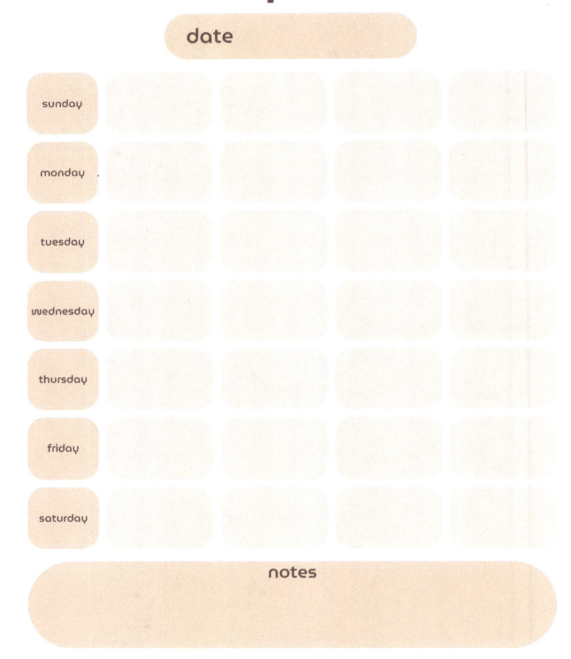

sunday

monday

tuesday

wednesday

thursday

friday

saturday

notes

NOTE SOMETHING DOWN

Made in the USA
Las Vegas, NV
10 April 2025

20758887R00044